CAN GOD BE SEEN IN OTHER WAYS

Hymns and Tunes for Today

Texts and Tunes by
John Thornburg
and
Jane Marshall

Abingdon Press
Nashville

Foreword

Here are two hymnists who deserve each other, in the best sense of that phrase. They are both soaked in hymnic lore, their craft is secure, and their ideas mesh and support one another. Both are blessed with intelligence, taste, and a willingness to explore paths that are "less traveled by." John tackles meaningful subjects in brief lines that often offer a jolt of surprise. Jane is incapable of writing an unsingable tune. And when they change places in "Constant Need," we see again that poetic and musical lyricism must be two sides of the same coin; how else could they do it so gracefully?

The hymns sing of God and the devil, of Israelites in the desert and the church in the inner city. They note our need for prophets who can "convert strife to life," or, like "holy thorns," turn us from our careless ways. The music ranges from sweet ballads to strong marches, from a drunken Noah in 7/8 to a chromatic "crafty foe," while "Two Mournful Men" drag slowly on their way to the risen Christ. There is a lovely, characteristic use of sequence, which often lands us on an unexpected cadence. There is a variety of meters, from a deft use of familiar forms to such intricate oddities as 95.55.66.11 ("Birth Is a Door").

Many of the songs are to be sung in unison, with a page included for congregational use. The poems are printed separately; all the harmonized versions are within the grasp of a good amateur keyboard player. Not one hymn is trite, or treats a conventional subject in polite language. Each tune and text speaks to the mind and heart—and most surely to the human voices who will want to sing them all.

Alice Parker

Contents

The Hymns (Page No.)

1. Can God Be Seen in Other Ways (4)
2. Birth Is a Door (7)
3. Now Is the Time to See (10)
4. The Puddles Lingered on the Earth (13)
5. The Dawn of Life, the Breath of God (17)
6. Still Breathless from Their Flight (20)
7. The Tiny Feathered Pilgrim (22)
8. When Mary Searched for Words (25)
9. Blessed Is He Who Comes in God's Name (29)
10. An Unexpected Guest Arrived (32)
11. The Crafty Foe (34)
12. No Matter What Good Sense We Own (36)
13. Two Mournful Men (39)
14. When Cities Change (43)
15. We Search in Vain (46)
16. When Faith and Culture Clash (48)

Metrical Index (51)

Topical Index (52)

Scripture Index (54)

The Hymn Tunes (Page No.)

ENGLISH (5)

THE DOOR (8)

BLANTON (11)

DECISION (14)

NEW DAY (18)

GRATITUDE (21)

SHELTER (23)

MARYSONG (26)

LAMENT (30)

HEART'S PERFUME (33)

CONFRONTATION (35)

CONSTANT NEED (37)

OPENED EYES (40)

COUNTERPLOT (44)

NEW WORLD (47)

McELVANEY (49)

Can God Be Seen in Other Ways

Can God be seen in other ways
than crowned and seated on a throne?
Is God the source of matchless might,
immovable as age-old stone?

Or could it be that God is glimpsed
in ordinary time and space,
a sovereign not remote at all
but seen in every human face?

In those evicted by the world,
the aging man, the refugee,
the woman, used and then abused,
God's image we can clearly see.

In all with crushed and splintered dreams
who look for little from above,
the Holy One seeks out and dwells
with steadfast, hope-producing love.

WORDS: John Thornburg
© 2003 Abingdon Press, admin. by The Copyright Co.

Duplication without permission is strictly prohibited.

This hymn was commissioned for the 10th anniversary of North Dallas Shared Ministries, an ecumenical relief agency in Dallas. I felt it would be a good idea to talk with the agency's director, the Rev. Matt English, to get his reflections. In the midst of that conversation, I asked Matt to reflect on the faith of those who came for assistance. "Well," he said, "they certainly have splintered dreams." The tune was named ENGLISH to honor Matt's ministry. JT

Can God Be Seen in Other Ways

1. Can God be seen in oth-er ways than crowned and seat-ed on a throne? Is God the source of match-less might, im-mov-a-ble as age-old stone?
2. Or could it be that God is glimpsed in or-di-nar-y time and space, a sov-'reign not re-mote at all but seen in ev-ery hu-man face?
3. In all e-vict-ed by the world, the a-ging man, the ref-u-gee, the wo-man, used and then a-bused, God's im-age we can clear-ly see.
4. In those with crushed and splin-tered dreams who look for lit-tle from a-bove, the Ho-ly One seeks out and dwells with stead-fast, hope-pro-duc-ing love.

WORDS: John Thornburg
MUSIC: Jane Marshall
© 2003 Abingdon Press, admin. by The Copyright Co.

Duplication without permission is strictly prohibited.

Birth Is a Door

Birth is a door to color and sound, to life all around;
the earth and the sky, the wet and the dry;
the need for affection, the threat of rejection;
the search for the story that gives us a name.

Life is a door to joy and to pain, to sunshine and rain;
the summons to serve, the failure of nerve;
the need for vocation, for godly formation;
the urge to be numbered as faithful and just.

Death is a door to wholeness and peace, to rest and release;
where tears are no more, where trust is the core;
no winning and losing, no strife or accusing;
but God, the beginning, the middle, the end.

WORDS: John Thornburg
© 2003 Abingdon Press, admin. by The Copyright Co.
Duplication without permission is strictly prohibited.

Jane and I received a commission from Kessler Park United Methodist Church, Dallas, for a children's anthem to honor that church's longtime children's choir director, Betty Zumwalt. Betty had endured a long battle with cancer with enormous grace and was a great inspiration to the congregation.

Because Betty was near death when we received the commission, my thoughts gravitated to the whole notion of death as a threshold, and to the faith conviction that God stood on both sides of that threshold. I worked with the image of the door, but realized that death was not the only threshold event in the Christian life. Though this is not the text we decided upon for the children's anthem, it was an important part of the journey to finding the right text for children. JT

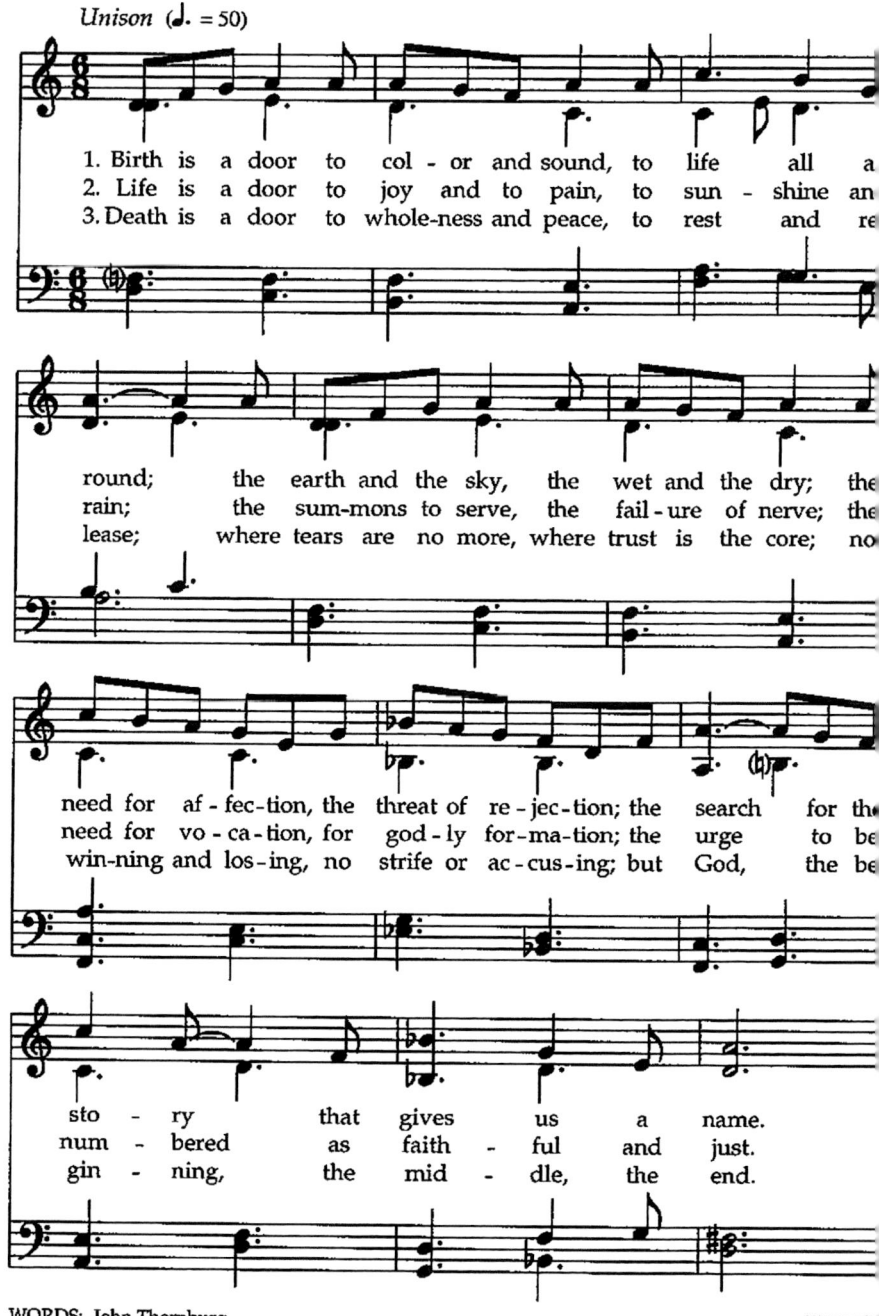

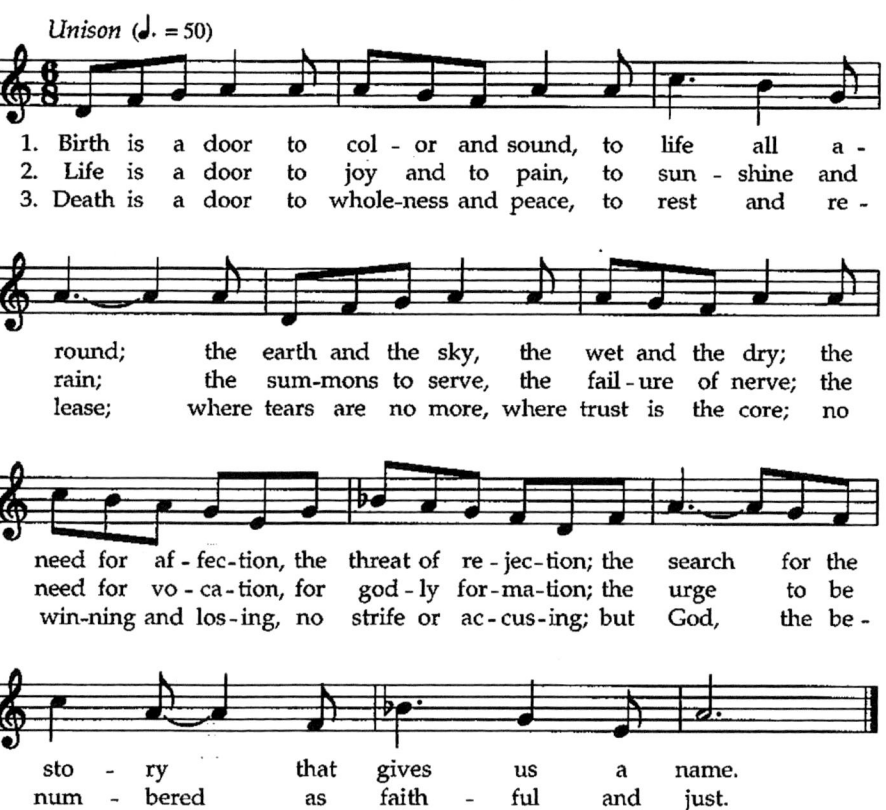

For the 20th anniversary of the ordination of Dr. Georjean Blanton

Now Is the Time to See

Now is the time to see
God's own distinctive artistry,
shaping the now and yet to be;

> *Refrain*
> Now is the perfect time.
> Now is the moment.

Now is the time to weep;
apathy conquers, yet we sleep,
mocking the ones whose pain is deep;

> *Refrain*

Now is the time to turn,
guided by grace we cannot earn,
making God's love our sole concern;

> *Refrain*

Now is the time to grow,
stretching the bounds of what we know,
choosing the steadfast way to go;

> *Refrain*

WORDS: John Thornburg
© 2003 Abingdon Press, admin. by The Copyright Co.
Duplication without permission is strictly prohibited.

This text honored Dr. Georjean Blanton, pastor of Preston Hollow United Methodist Church in Dallas. When I received an invitation to a celebration marking the 20th anniversary of Georjean's ordination, I knew that I wanted to write a hymn text for the occasion. I had also written a text for the wedding of Georjean and her husband, Mike Renquist. I hoped to weave the pastoral and prophetic dimensions of ministry into this text to pay tribute to Georjean's skillful and loving combination of those dimensions in her ministry. The first draft of the text began, "There is a time …," but Jane suggested the strength and immediacy of the word "now." JT

The Puddles Lingered on the Earth

The puddles lingered on the earth, reminders of the flood;
then signals of the Gardener's work came poking through the mud.
The builder of the saving ark, the father of three sons,
began to till the virgin soil; a vineyard was begun.

Then Noah took those primal grapes; he pressed them into wine.
And soon, in drunken stupor, fell, his bearings undermined.
His sons beheld his naked frame, uncovered in his tent.
So Chapter One of "After Flood" was grist for God's lament.

Are we the heirs, the scions of that drunken patriarch,
when we step out upon the deck of our own saving ark?
Will we rebuke the covenant, God's act of lavish grace,
or claim the rainbow promise now in our own time and place?

WORDS: John Thornburg (Gen. 9:20-28)
© 2003 Abingdon Press, admin. by The Copyright Co.

Duplication without permission is strictly prohibited.

Though originally intending to write a text about the Tower of Babel story in Genesis 11, I backed up a few chapters in Genesis to get the context. The more I read the story of Noah's post-flood drunkenness, the more I realized that I'd like to address the whole issue of fumbling the promise of God. The challenge in the poem is to capture the tragic/comic dimensions of the story. As in "Still Breathless from Their Flight," I wanted to capture the notion of what happened right after the flood, and so I imagined that if there's that much water on the earth, there would have to be puddles. JT

The Puddles Lingered on the Earth

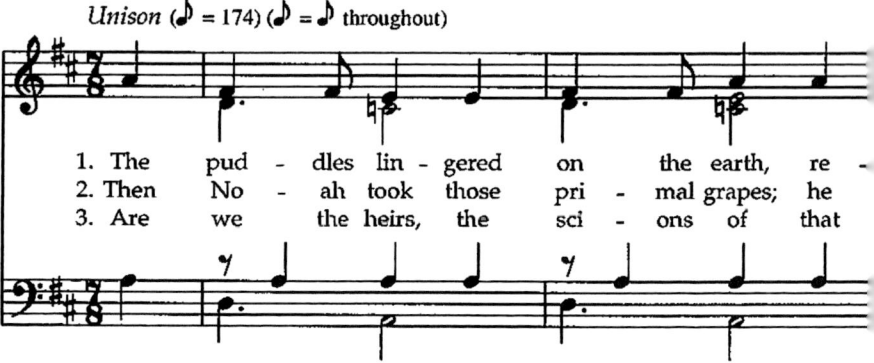

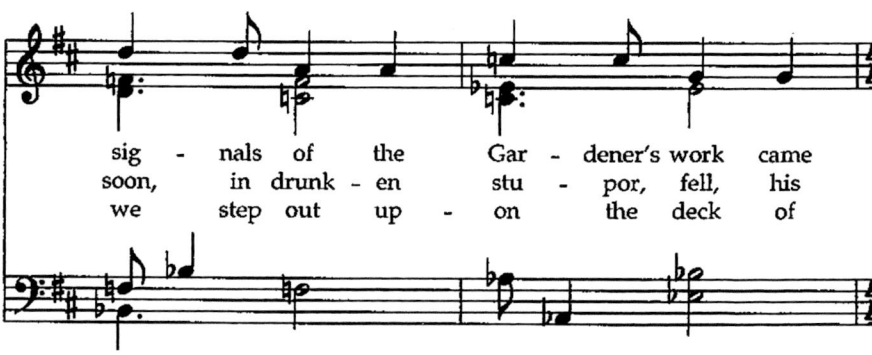

WORDS: John Thornburg (Gen. 9:20-28)
MUSIC: Jane Marshall
© 2003 Abingdon Press, admin. by The Copyright Co.

DECISIC
CM

Duplication without permission is strictly prohibited.

The Dawn of Life, the Breath of God

The dawn of life, the breath of God —
the morning dew on Eden's sod —
earth's Builder toiled, made heaven here.
The human pair succumbed to fear:
disputed fruit took root.

From Babel's tower to Jacob's tricks —
the broken things no glue can fix —
yet even so, the God of grace
keeps showing up in every place,
converting strife to life.

The time will come, the precious day
when all our No's will pass away
and God will use our hands to bless.
Our lips will sing a joyous Yes!
exchanging schemes for dreams.

WORDS: John Thornburg
© 2003 Abingdon Press, admin. by The Copyright Co.
Duplication without permission is strictly prohibited.

Working from the conviction that God is dripping with sweat from loving us despite our failings, I wanted to offer images of God's goodness juxtaposed with our cluelessness and fear. This text may be quite "American" given that in other English speaking countries the word "scheme" does not necessarily have the negative connotations that it does in the United States. The phrase "exchanging schemes for dreams" is meant to tie most immediately to the reference to "Jacob's tricks." Through most of my childhood, I heard Sunday school teachers refer to Jacob as a "schemer." JT

The Dawn of Life, the Breath of God

WORDS: John Thornburg
MUSIC: Jane Marshall
© 2003 Abingdon Press, admin. by The Copyright Co.

NEW DAY
88.88.6

Duplication without permission is strictly prohibited.

Still Breathless from Their Flight

Still breathless from their flight,
with sea-sand on their feet,
the favored people, freedom won,
found God's love incomplete.

"What shall we drink?" they whined,
when Marah's water proved
to be as bitter as their tone.
So clueless and unmoved!

Then Moses cried to God,
so God showed him a tree;
which, when he hurled the branches in,
made briny waters sweet.

Is this our story, too?
Are we all "moan and fuss"?
Which modern Moses do we ask
to intercede for us?

We thank you, patient God,
despite our frequent cries.
May we enjoy the drink of life
that you alone supply.

WORDS: John Thornburg
© 2003 Abingdon Press, admin. by The Copyright Co.

Duplication without permission is strictly prohibited.

I've always been curious about what happened right after the great events narrated in scripture. What was it like for Elijah coming down from the mountaintop after hearing the still, small voice? What did the nine lepers who didn't return to thank Jesus do? In the case of Exodus 15, we actually have this brilliant description of what the Hebrews did after the Exodus. I wanted to capture that sense of *right after* and so I pictured myself walking up out of the semi-murky stuff through which the Hebrews walked to freedom. I simply imagined myself as breathless. JT

Still Breathless from Their Flight

WORDS: John Thornburg (Ex. 15:22-27)
MUSIC: Jane Marshall
2003 Abingdon Press, admin. by The Copyright Co.
Duplication without permission is strictly prohibited.

GRATITUDE
SM

The Tiny Feathered Pilgrim

The tiny feathered pilgrim has found a place to rest;
the temple pillars beckon; they offer her some rest.

The need for sheltered solace so deep within her breast
is met among these columns. She is the Maker's guest.

Now other pilgrims enter on feet instead of wings.
But they, too, ache for welcome and for the hope it brings.

Once settled in the courtyard where alleluias ring,
the pilgrims can surrender. The faithful boldly sing,

"How lovely is your dwelling, O Lord of all that lives!
My soul yearns for a refuge; the shelter that you give."

WORDS: John Thornburg (Ps. 84)
© 2003 Abingdon Press, admin. by The Copyright Co.

Duplication without permission is strictly prohibited.

I have a bird feeder right outside the window of the room in which I do most of my writing, and there is a sparrow convention most mornings around 11:00. I had decided that I wanted to do at least one psalm paraphrase for this collection, and on the day that I set about to choose a psalm, sparrows from all over North Texas showed up in the backyard, so I took it as a sign that Psalm 84 was the one! JT

The Tiny Feathered Pilgrim

Unison (♩. = 50)

1. The ti - ny feath - ered pil - grim has found a place to rest; the tem - ple pil - lars beck - on; they of - fer her some rest.
2. The need for shel - tered so - lace so deep with-in her breast is met a - mong these col - umns. She is the Mak - er's guest.
3. Now oth - er pil - grims en - ter on feet in-stead of wings. But they, too, ache for wel - come and for the hope it brings.
4. Once set - tled in the court - yard where al - le - lu - ias ring, the pil - grims can sur - ren - der. The faith - ful bold - ly sing,
5. "How love - ly is your dwell - ing, O Lord of all that lives! My soul yearns for a ref - uge; the shel - ter that you give."

WORDS: John Thornburg (Ps. 84)
MUSIC: Jane Marshall
© 2003 Abingdon Press, admin. by The Copyright Co.

SHELTER
76.76

Duplication without permission is strictly prohibited.

The Tiny Feathered Pilgrim

(𝅗𝅥. = 50)

1. The tiny feathered pilgrim has found a place to rest; the temple pillars beckon; they offer her some rest.
2. The need for sheltered solace so deep within her breast is met among these columns. She is the Maker's guest.
3. Now other pilgrims enter on feet instead of wings. But they, too, ache for welcome and for the hope it brings.
4. Once settled in the courtyard where alleluias ring, the pilgrims can sunder. The faithful boldly sing,
5. "How lovely is your dwelling, O Lord of all that lives! My soul yearns for a refuge; the shelter that you give."

WORDS: John Thornburg (Ps. 84)
MUSIC: Jane Marshall
© 2003 Abingdon Press, admin. by The Copyright Co.

SHELTI
76.

Duplication without permission is strictly prohibited.

When Mary Searched for Words

When Mary searched for words
to capture what her spirit knew,
she glorified the One
who turned familiar things askew.

"Our way is this," she said.
"The mighty have the highest place.
But God's own sense of height
requires the lowly to be raised."

"God feeds the hungry ones;
the rich are left with emptiness.
And Israel and her heirs
God will forever richly bless."

WORDS: John Thornburg (Lk. 1:39-56)
© 2003 Abingdon Press, admin. by The Copyright Co.

Duplication without permission is strictly prohibited.

In much the same way that I felt called to write a psalm paraphrase for this collection (see "The Tiny Feathered Pilgrim"), I felt that it was time for me to attempt a paraphrase of the Magnificat. In the midst of it all, I came to realize just how challenging it is to paraphrase something that intense and beloved. JT

When Mary Searched for Words

WORDS: John Thornburg (Lk. 1:39-56)
MUSIC: Jane Marshall

© 2003 Abingdon Press, admin. by The Copyright Co.
Duplication without permission is strictly prohibited.

MARYSON
68.

When Mary Searched for Words

WORDS: John Thornburg (Lk. 1:39-56)
MUSIC: Jane Marshall
© 2003 Abingdon Press, admin. by The Copyright Co.

MARYSON
68.6

Duplication without permission is strictly prohibited.

Blessed Is He Who Comes in God's Name

"Blessed is he who comes in God's name!"
cried the excited crowd.
Spreading their cloaks, they welcomed a "King";
"Peace," they said, "here and now!"

As the great city came into view
Jesus began to cry.
"Would that you knew the makings of peace!"
he uttered with a sigh.

They did not hear him; neither do we.
Might is our golden calf.
We would see Christ equipped with a sword,
not with a shepherd's staff.

Peace is not gained through posture and threat.
Justice is not a game.
Come, Christians, turn; surrender the pride;
repent in Jesus' name.

WORDS: John Thornburg (Lk. 19:28-47)
© 2003 Abingdon Press, admin. by The Copyright Co.

Duplication without permission is strictly prohibited.

This hymn was the result of a reversal of our normal collaborative process. We usually begin with text and allow it to suggest the musical ideas. In this case, Jane had written the tune LAMENT for a poem of mine about the pain of broken relationships. Since I loved the tune, I asked myself what Bible story had the kind of feeling suggested in its melodic line. I considered different stories, but always came back to Jesus' lament over Jerusalem. JT

Blessed Is He Who Comes in God's Name

WORDS: John Thornburg (Lk. 19:28-47)
MUSIC: Jane Marshall
© 2003 Abingdon Press, admin. by The Copyright Co.
Duplication without permission is strictly prohibited.

Blessed Is He Who Comes in God's Name

Unison (𝅗𝅥. = 42, in two)

1. "Bless-ed is he who comes in God's name!"
2. As the great cit-y came in-to view
3. They did not hear him; nei-ther do we.
4. Peace is not gained through pos-ture and threat.

   cried the ex-cit-ed crowd.
   Je-sus be-gan to cry.
   Might is our gold-en calf.
   Jus-tice is not a game.

Spread-ing their cloaks, they wel-comed a "King";
"Would that you knew the mak-ings of peace!"
We would see Christ e-quipped with a sword,
Come, Chris-tians, turn; sur-ren-der the pride;

"Peace," they said, "here and now!"
he ut-tered with a sigh.
not with a shep-herd's staff.
re-pent in Je-sus' name.

WORDS: John Thornburg (Lk. 19:28-47)
MUSIC: Jane Marshall
© 2003 Abingdon Press, admin. by The Copyright Co.

LAMENT
96.96

Duplication without permission is strictly prohibited.

An Unexpected Guest Arrived

An unexpected guest arrived
at Simon's modest dining room.
She brought two different gifts that day;
an act of care and sweet perfume.

They stood aghast, then spoke with rage,
"How dare she waste a gift so dear?"
Then Jesus said, "She understands.
You will not always have me here."

Her lavish act of ministry,
rejected by their pious wrath,
ignites the hope and calms the fear
of those who seek the servant path.

She is a saint, this nameless one,
a mentor in our own rebirth.
Now, will we keep the Savior's vow
and make her known throughout the earth?

WORDS: John Thornburg (Mk. 14:3-9)
© 2003 Abingdon Press, admin. by The Copyright Co.
Duplication without permission is strictly prohibited.

This text was inspired by a sermon preached at Northaven United Methodist Church, Dallas, by Professor Marjorie Proctor-Smith of Perkins School of Theology. She pointed out that the church had failed to carry out the promise of Jesus that the faith of the woman who anointed Jesus would be remembered wherever the gospel is preached (Mark 14:9).

As a result of that sermon, Northaven's worship committee asked how the church could attempt to keep Jesus' promise. The members decided that because the woman's anointing of Jesus had prepared him for what was ahead (*i.e.*, his death), all those baptized at Northaven would be offered the ritual of anointing to prepare them for what was ahead (dying and being raised in baptism). JT

The Crafty Foe

The crafty foe that Jesus faced
when summoned to the tempting place prepared his ploys.
That tempter scoffed, "Turn stones to bread."
"I'll heed the word of God instead," the Savior said.

From Satan's tongue then came a dare:
"Surrender to your angel's care; dive through the air!"
But Jesus scorned the hellish prod
and answered back, his spine a rod, "Do not tempt God!"

Yet Satan said, "What you can see
is yours if you will bend the knee and worship me."
The Lord of Life, nerve strong as stone,
cried, "God I'll serve, heart, mind and bone, and God alone."

WORDS: John Thornburg (Mt. 4:1-11)
© 2003 Abingdon Press, admin. by The Copyright Co.

Duplication without permission is strictly prohibited.

In the middle 1980s, I heard a brilliant sermon by James Forbes at Riverside Church in New York entitled "How Long Did Jesus Wait?" In that sermon, Forbes asked how long Jesus waited before responding to each of the temptations placed before him by the devil. That inquiry in Forbes' sermon became a very important part of my continuing faith journey because, at some level, the way we answer that question tells us whether we are more attracted to and motivated by the human Jesus or the divine Jesus. Are the offers of the devil called temptations because they actually caused *Jesus* some pause, or are they called temptations only because they would sorely test *us*? JT

No Matter What Good Sense We Own

No matter what good sense we own
or what brave hearts we've shown;
no matter how our faith has grown,
we need you still, O Lord.

Whatever pride we've recognized,
yet prayed it be re-sized;
whatever gains we've realized,
we need you still, O Lord.

Despite our tendency to doubt,
then put distrust to rout;
however loud the praise we shout,
we need you still, O Lord.

Regardless of our creaturehood,
that mix of would or should;
we seek you as all-loving Good,
and need you still, O Lord.

WORDS: Jane Marshall
© 2003 Abingdon Press, admin. by The Copyright Co.
Duplication without permission is strictly prohibited.

Cultures and societies may have changed since the ancient Hebrews' deliverance from Egypt, Babylon, and other areas of trouble, but human nature seems to be very much what it was for our ancestors. We encounter problems, deliverance, then self-centered forgetfulness of God's goodness—the latter particularly when life is running smoothly—just as the Hebrews did. I observe such behavior in myself all the time, and this hymn is simply a way of going public with it.

It is also the one hymn in this collection in which John and I reverse roles: here he is the composer, I the poet. It was pure fun seeing whether we could do it. JM

No Matter What Good Sense We Own

1. No matter what good sense we own or what brave hearts we've shown; no matter how our faith has grown, we need you still, O Lord.
2. Whatever pride we've recognized, yet prayed it be resized; whatever gains we've realized, we need you still, O Lord.
3. Despite our tendency to doubt, then put distrust to rout; however loud the praise we shout, we need you still, O Lord.
4. Regardless of our creaturehood, that mix of would or should; we seek you as all-loving Good, and need you still, O Lord.

WORDS: Jane Marshall
MUSIC: John Thornburg
2003 Abingdon Press, admin. by The Copyright Co.

CONSTANT NEED
CM

Duplication without permission is strictly prohibited.

No Matter What Good Sense We Own

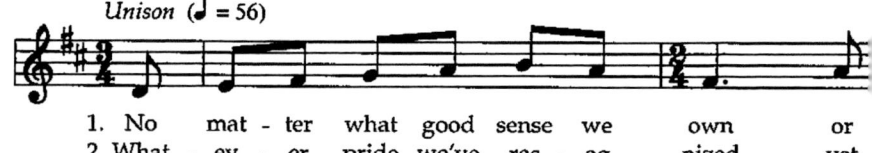

1. No mat-ter what good sense we own or
2. What-ev-er pride we've rec-og-nized, yet
3. De-spite our ten-den-cy to doubt, then
4. Re-gard-less of our crea-ture-hood, that

what brave hearts we've shown; no mat-ter how our faith has
prayed it be re-sized; what-ev-er gains we've re-al-
put dis-trust to rout; how-ev-er loud the praise we
mix of would or should; we seek you as all-lov-ing

grown, we need you still, O Lord.
ized, we need you still, O Lord.
shout, we need you still, O Lord.
Good, and need you still, O Lord.

WORDS: Jane Marshall
MUSIC: John Thornburg
© 2003 Abingdon Press, admin. by The Copyright Co.

CONSTANT N

Duplication without permission is strictly prohibited.

Two Mournful Men

Two mournful men walked seven miles.
Their hopes were dashed, their eyes were down.
The cross had splintered all their hopes.

Then Jesus came and walked with them.
Their teary eyes still raked the ground.
The journey home brought no relief.

He questioned them about the news.
They answered him, "Have you not heard:
our Savior, dead; his body, gone?"

With forthright voice he counterclaimed:
"It had to be that he should die."
The mourners still were unaware.

With home in sight they bade him stay.
With table set he broke the bread,
and then, by grace, they recognized.

With open eyes and ransomed hearts
they went and told that Jesus lived.
What miracles in broken bread!

WORDS: John Thornburg (Lk. 24:13-35)
© 2003 Abingdon Press, admin. by The Copyright Co.
Duplication without permission is strictly prohibited.

It was through Jane's patient mentoring that I came to realize the challenge facing the hymn tune writer when the text changes moods. So the story of the road to Emmaus offers a distinctive challenge. If you're going to be true to the biblical story, you have to start where the two travelers do, with eyes downcast, and end where they do, in joyful amazement. So how grateful I am to have a tune writer who has faced this challenge so many times before and painted a musical picture that allows for those moods. JT

Two Mournful Men

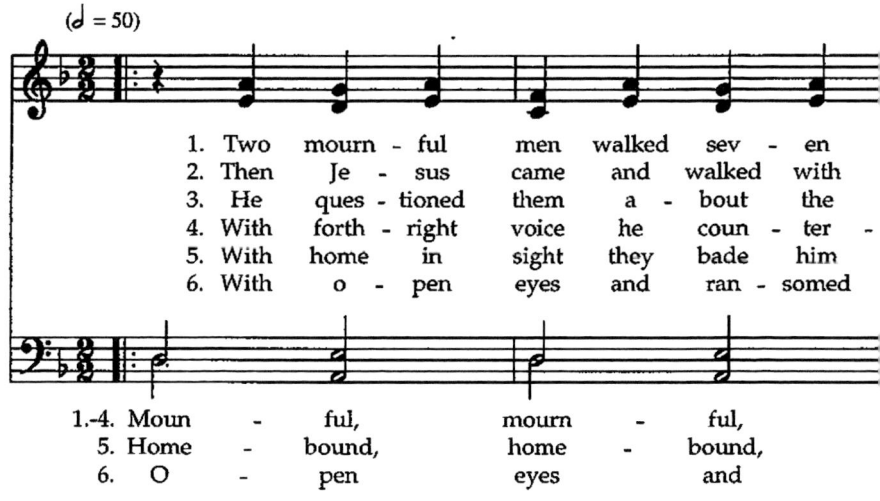

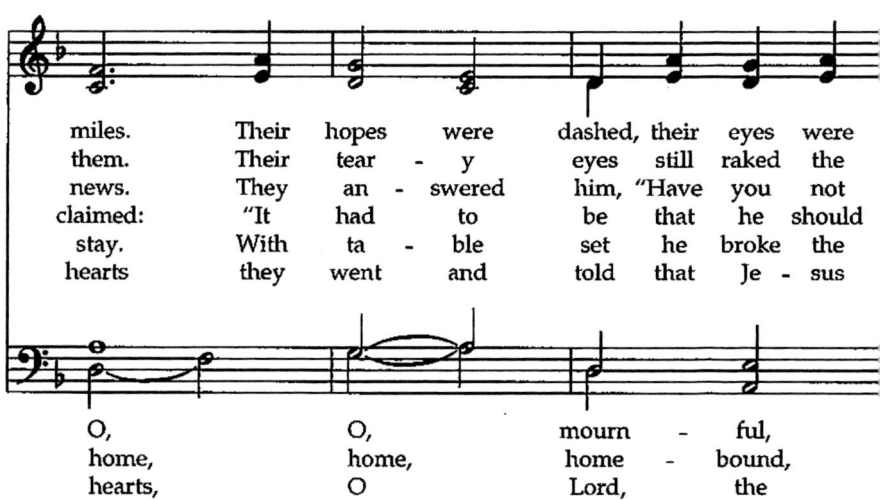

WORDS: John Thornburg (Lk. 24:13-35)
MUSIC: Jane Marshall
© 2003 Abingdon Press, admin. by The Copyright Co.

OPENED EY]
44.44

Duplication without permission is strictly prohibited.

Two Mournful Men

($\quarternote$ = 50)

1. Two mourn-ful men walked sev-en miles. Their hopes were dashed, their eyes were down. The cross had splin-tered all their hopes.
2. Then Je-sus came and walked with them. Their tear-y eyes still raked the ground. The jour-ney home brought no re-lief.
3. He ques-tioned them a-bout the news. They an-swered him, "Have you not heard: our Sav-ior, dead; his bod-y, gone?"
4. With forth-right voice he coun-ter-claimed: "It had to be that he should die." The mourn-ers still were un-a-ware.
5. With home in sight they bade him stay. With ta-ble set he broke the bread, and then, by grace, they re-cog-nized.
6. With o-pen eyes and ran-somed hearts they went and told that Je-sus lived. What mir-a-cles in bro-ken bread!

WORDS: John Thornburg (Lk. 24:13-35)
MUSIC: Jane Marshall
© 2003 Abingdon Press, admin. by The Copyright Co.
Duplication without permission is strictly prohibited.

OPENED EY
44.4

42

When Cities Change

When cities change and neighborhoods become a whole new blend,
the God who made each vibrant face envisions us as friends.

When needle, knife, and bullet slug adorn the church's lot,
the God who aches and works for peace creates a counterplot.

The plot is this: despite our view that "church" must fit a mold,
the God who wrecks dividing walls commands us to be bold.

Extend the plot, Eternal God; place us within the tale.
Encourage us to live the hope that you alone unveil.

WORDS: John Thornburg
© 2003 Abingdon Press, admin. by The Copyright Co.
Duplication without permission is strictly prohibited.

This text was written to mark the 20th anniversary of the founding of a fifteen-church coalition called the East Dallas Cooperative Parish. The parish was founded to breathe life into six United Methodist churches that had been the suburban cathedrals of Dallas Methodism in the 1920s through the 1950s. Each church had encountered the familiar challenge of ministering to an ethnically diverse and poverty-stricken neighborhood. Through visionary leadership and durability of sainthood, the churches reclaimed a vital mission in their neighborhoods. The parish has grown to include Southern Baptist, Episcopalian, Presbyterian, Lutheran, UCC, and Disciples of Christ congregations, as well as an independent congregation with a primary outreach to the gay community. JT

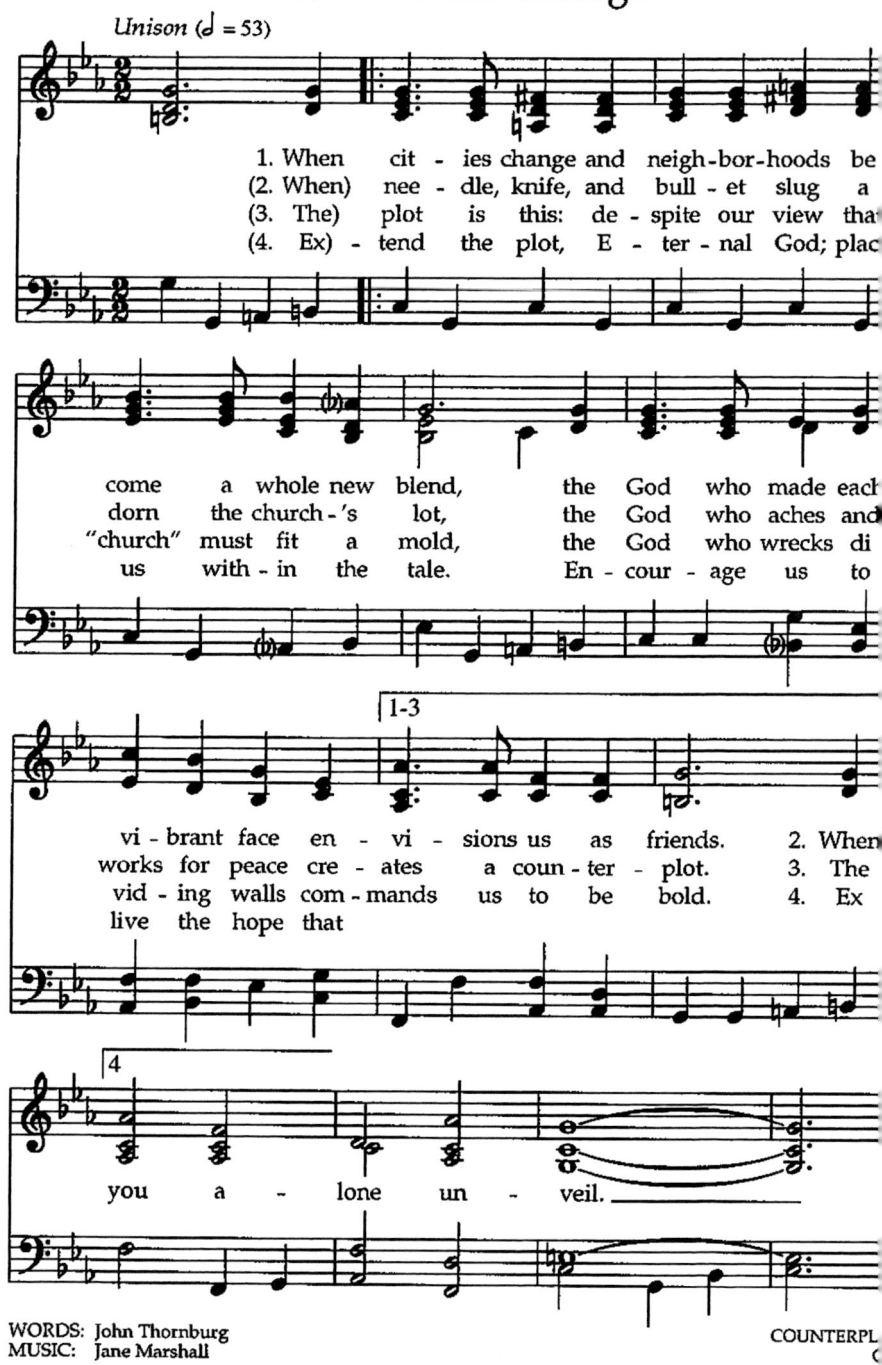

When Cities Change

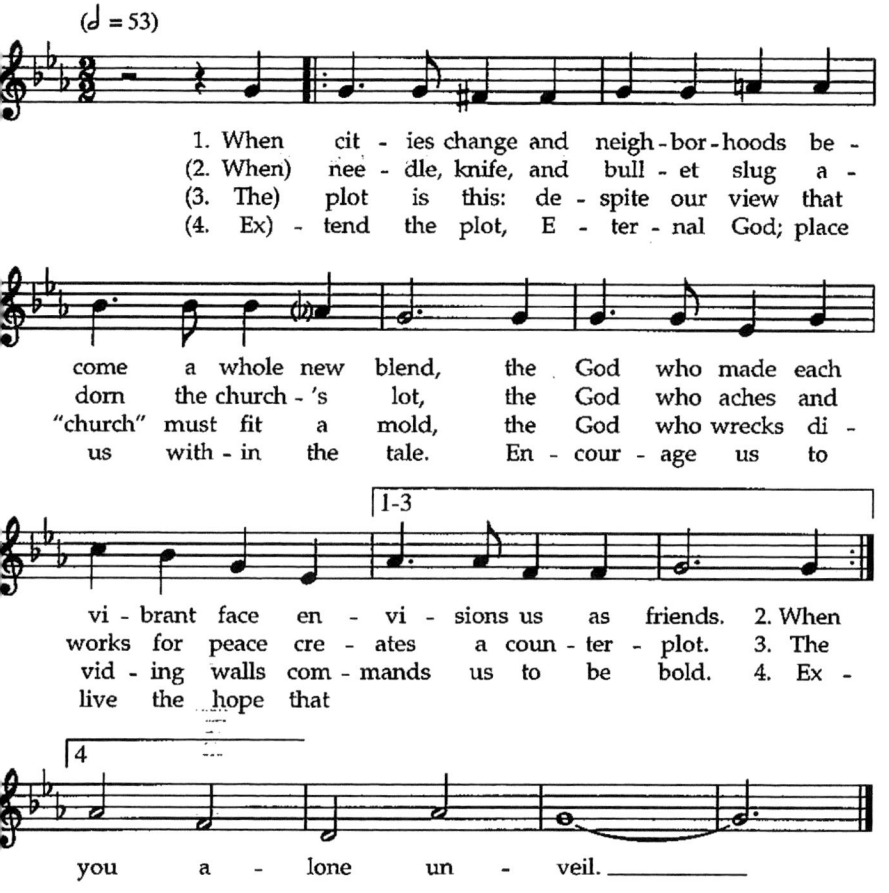

1. When cities change and neighborhoods become a whole new blend, the God who made each vibrant face envisions us as friends.
(2. When) needle, knife, and bullet slug adorn the church-'s lot, the God who aches and works for peace creates a counter-plot.
(3. The) plot is this: despite our view that "church" must fit a mold, the God who wrecks dividing walls commands us to be bold.
(4. Ex)tend the plot, Eternal God; place us within the tale. Encourage us to live the hope that you alone unveil.

WORDS: John Thornburg
MUSIC: Jane Marshall
2003 Abingdon Press, admin. by The Copyright Co.

COUNTERPLOT
CM

Duplication without permission is strictly prohibited.

We Search in Vain

We search in vain: we think we know
the way to happiness.
We think it leads through wealth and fame,
as if to purchase bliss.

The more we claim that life is ours
to shape and quantify,
the more we come to realize
that we have lived a lie.

But then the God who never sleeps,
the One who raised the dead,
speaks up and says the freeing word,
"Come follow me instead."

And when we feel that holy nudge,
and claim the call as ours,
it is as though the world is new;
our prison has no bars.

WORDS: John Thornburg
© 2003 Abingdon Press, admin. by The Copyright Co.
Duplication without permission is strictly prohibited.

The city of Dallas, with all its wonders and blemishes, has been the setting for my whole ministry. While there is a "can-do" spirit and a lot of entrepreneurial energy within Dallas, there is also an all-too-vibrant spirit of conspicuous consumption. I wrote this text shortly after fire destroyed a house in North Dallas that was a few weeks away from completion. When completed, this house was to have had 75,000 square feet and be valued at $45 million. JT

When Faith and Culture Clash

When faith and culture clash, when church collides with state,
an agent for authentic love must rise to challenge hate.

When people call for war and hunger for a fight,
God's prophets must emerge and speak to break inertia's might.

A renegade for peace, a midwife for the truth:
we ache, O God, for one to act as justice-seeking sleuth.

Praise God for all like these, who scandalize our scorn
and perforate our prejudice, each one a holy thorn.

WORDS: John Thornburg
© 2003 Abingdon Press, admin. by The Copyright Co.
Duplication without permission is strictly prohibited.

This text was written to honor the prophetic ministry of Rev. William K. McElvaney on the occasion of his retirement from the faculty of Perkins School of Theology in Dallas. Bill had been a pastor in the North Texas Conference, including a six-year ministry at Northaven United Methodist Church, the church at which Jane is a long-time member and where I served as pastor for 10 years (1991-2001). Bill then served for 15 years as President of St. Paul School of Theology in Kansas City before returning to Dallas to teach worship and preaching at Perkins. JT

When Faith and Culture Clash

1. When faith and cul-ture clash, when church col-lides with
2. When peo-ple call for war and hun-ger for a
3. A ren-e-gade for peace, a mid-wife for the
4. Praise God for all like these, who scan-dal-ize our

state, an a - gent for au-
fight, God's proph - ets must e-
truth: we ache, O God, for
scorn and per - fo - rate our

then - tic love must rise to chal - lenge hate.
merge and speak to break in - er - tia's might.
one to act as jus - tice - seek - ing sleuth.
pre - ju - dice, each one a ho - ly thorn.

WORDS: John Thornburg
MUSIC: Jane Marshall
2003 Abingdon Press, admin. by The Copyright Co.
Duplication without permission is strictly prohibited.

McELVANEY
SM

When Faith and Culture Clash

1. When faith and culture clash, when church collides with state, an agent for authentic love must rise to challenge hate.
2. When people call for war and hunger for a fight, God's prophets must emerge and speak to break inertia's might.
3. A renegade for peace, a midwife for the truth: we ache, O God, for one to act as justice-seeking sleuth.
4. Praise God for all like these, who scandalize our scorn and perforate our prejudice, each one a holy thorn.

WORDS: John Thornburg
MUSIC: Jane Marshall
© 2003 Abingdon Press, admin. by The Copyright Co.

McELVANE
S

Duplication without permission is strictly prohibited.

Metrical Index

SM (66.86)
    GRATITUDE (21)
    McELVANEY (49)

CM (86.86)
    CONSTANT NEED (37)
    COUNTERPLOT (44)
    NEW WORLD (47)

CMD (86.86 D)
    DECISION (14)

LM (88.88)
    ENGLISH (5)
    HEART'S PERFUME (33)

44.44.8
    OPENED EYES (40)

68.68
    MARYSONG (26)

688 with Refrain
    BLANTON (11)

76.76
    SHELTER (23)

884.884
    CONFRONTATION (35)

88.88.6
    NEW DAY (18)

96.96
    LAMENT (30)

Irregular
    THE DOOR (8)

Topical Index

Theme	Title (Page No.)
Apathy	Now Is the Time to See (10)
Bold Faith	An Unexpected Guest Arrived (32)
Christian Growth	Now Is the Time to See (10)
Church and State	When Faith and Culture Clash (48)
Eucharist	Two Mournful Men (39)
Faith and Doubt	No Matter What Good Sense We Own (36)
Freedom	We Search in Vain (46)
God, Call of	We Search in Vain (46)
Covenant	The Puddles Lingered on the Earth (13)
Creative Artistry	Now Is the Time to See (10)
Grace of	Now Is the Time to See (10) The Dawn of Life, the Breath of God (17) When Cities Change (43)
Justice of	When Mary Searched for Words (25) When Faith and Culture Clash (48)
Nature of	Can God Be Seen in Other Ways (4)
Patience	Still Breathless from Their Flight (20)
Service to	The Crafty Foe (34)
Worship of	The Tiny Feathered Pilgrim (22)
Hope	When Cities Change (43) Can God Be Seen in Other Ways (4)
Human Condition	Still Breathless from Their Flight (20) The Dawn of Life, the Breath of God (17) The Puddles Lingered on the Earth (13)
Jesus' Life and Ministry	An Unexpected Guest Arrived (32) Blessed Is He Who Comes in God's Name (29) The Crafty Foe (34) Two Mournful Men (39)

Topical Index (continued)

Life in the City	When Cities Change (43)
Life's Passages	Birth Is a Door (7)
	Now Is the Time to See (10)
Miracle	Two Mournful Men (39)
Peace with Justice	Blessed Is He Who Comes in God's Name (29)
	When Faith and Culture Clash (48)
Pilgrimage	The Tiny Feathered Pilgrim (22)
Prophetic Ministry	When Faith and Culture Clash (48)
Refuge	The Tiny Feathered Pilgrim (22)
Temptation	The Crafty Foe (34)
Trust and Distrust	No Matter What Good Sense We Own (36)
Wealth	We Search in Vain (46)

PEOPLE

Jacob	The Dawn of Life, the Breath of God (17)
Mary	When Mary Searched for Words (25)
Moses	Still Breathless from Their Flight (20)
Noah	The Puddles Lingered on the Earth (13)
Satan	The Crafty Foe (34)
Simon	An Unexpected Guest Arrived (32)

PLACES

Babel	The Dawn of Life, the Breath of God (17)
Eden	The Dawn of Life, the Breath of God (17)
Emmaus	Two Mournful Men (39)
Marah	Still Breathless from Their Flight (20)

Scripture Index

Genesis
  9:20-28   The Puddles Lingered on the Earth (13)

Exodus
  15:22-27   Still Breathless from Their Flight (20)

Psalms
  84   The Tiny Feathered Pilgrim (22)

Matthew
  4:1-11   The Crafty Foe (34)

Mark
  14:3-9   An Unexpected Guest Arrived (32)

Luke
  1:39-56   When Mary Searched for Words (25)
  19:28-47   Blessed Is He Who Comes in God's Name (29)
  24:13-35   Two Mournful Men (39)